FAMILY ˈ
IN OXFORDSHIRE

Ten family outings around
Oxfordshire and its Borders

Georgina and Robert Neville

With Historical Notes

COUNTRYSIDE BOOKS
NEWBURY, BERKSHIRE

First Published 1983
© Georgina and Robert Neville 1983

COUNTRYSIDE BOOKS
3 Catherine Road,
Newbury, Berkshire
ISBN 0 905392 21 3

The authors would like to thank the
following for their help in the
preparation of this book:

Ivor Sweetnam for his photographic work

Pauline Sweetnam for her typing assistance

The Reverend Alan Pyburn for supplying
information about Remenham Church

Henley-on-Thames Public Library

Sketch maps by David Thelwell
Cover photograph by Fotobank England Scene
Printed in England by
Lovell Baines Print Ltd
Newbury, Berkshire

Contents

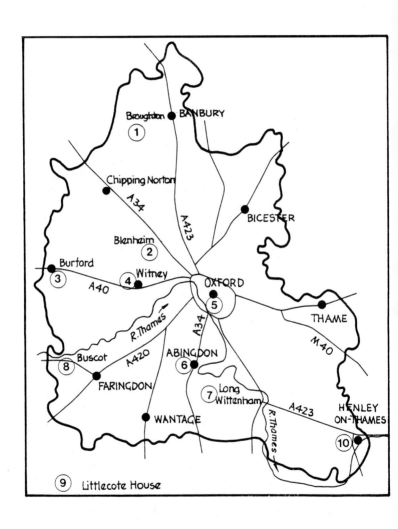

Introduction

The idea for this book emerged shortly after we became parents. We had previously enjoyed walking but realised that with a small child we would have to curtail some of the longer and more strenuous walks we had completed in the past. Accordingly, we began to explore routes which offered pleasant scenery, which were relatively short, which provided the family with the opportunity to visit places of interest, and which had adequate refreshments en route. We came to the conclusion that there were a large number of people in the same position who wished to take their children for walks which were easily manageable and which would cater for their special family needs.

This book is the result of our explorations and it presents a selection of circular walks in and around the beautiful county of Oxfordshire, which range from about 1½ to 4 miles in length, many of which can be completed in well under two hours. These walks are suitable for all ages; for the very young as well as for more elderly people wishing to undertake light walks and those taking up walking for the first time. Most of the routes follow good footpaths, some are on metalled tracks and wherever possible we have tried to avoid steep climbs and busy roads. In addition we have endeavoured to offer a wide range of walks affording a mixture of scenic beauty, historic interest, and family entertainment with adequate provision for refreshments or picnics. In these pages we not only present you with the freedom to enjoy a family walk in some of the most pleasant countryside in England, but also the chance to visit a Wild West Show, a moated castle, a Roman Villa, a haunted stately home, a wild life park, a farm museum, a miniature railway, and one of the most interesting university cities in the world.

Each walk includes information on how to reach the starting point by car, the length of the circuit, the names of nearby pubs, cafes and tea rooms, historical details of places to visit together with admission prices and opening times (please note that the latter are subject to change). In the text we have tried to give directions which are clear and very easy to follow. A sketch map accompanies each walk but it is often advisable to take an Ordnance Survey map with you.

Since many of the walks are near rivers and in some instances they follow roads for short distances, parents should naturally keep a firm control over young children unable to appreciate the possible dangers. We recommend the use of reins for very young children. Some, if not all, of the walks are quite suitable for pushchairs or buggies. It is advisable to wear a stout pair of shoes, for some stretches of the walks may be muddy after rain.

Finally, may we remind you of the Country Code:
— Guard against all risk of fire
— Fasten all gates
— Keep dogs under proper control
— Keep to paths across farm land
— Avoid damaging fences, hedges and walls
— Leave no litter
— Safeguard water supplies
— Protect wildlife, wild plants and trees
— Go carefully on country roads
— Respect the life of the countryside.

We hope that you will enjoy these walks and outings as much as we have done.

Georgina & Robert Neville
January 1983

Broughton Castle and the Saye and Sele Estate

Introduction: Broughton Castle (H.N.1), has an exquisite broad moat and is situated in beautiful parkland. It provides an ideal setting for an easy, leisurely afternoon's family walk. The castle is not a castle in the military sense, but is essentially an Elizabethan family home lived in by Lord and Lady Saye and Sele (H.N.2) and their family. The house with its remarkable contents is well worth visiting and the magnificent Great Hall contains arms and armour from the Civil War and other periods. Visitors may also see the castellated 15th century gatehouse and gardens together with the nearby Church of St. Mary (H.N.3). We recommend that you also wander through the extensive parkland and perhaps enjoy a picnic. For opening dates and times please see H.N.1.

Distance: This circular route is approximately 1¾ miles in length and should take about one hour to complete. Since the house and grounds are only open to the public for three hours (2pm-5pm) we suggest you arrive as near as possible to 2pm in order to enjoy both the walk and the visit to the house and grounds.

Refreshments: A tea room with home made teas is available for visitors to the house. Nearby in the village of Broughton is the Saye and Sele Arms public house which has gardens and lawns and serves good bar snacks and grills, but unfortunately not on Sundays.

How to get there: By car — Broughton Castle is two miles west of Banbury Cross on the B4035 Shipston-on-Stour/Banbury road. There is a free car park adjacent to the Church of St. Mary in the castle grounds.

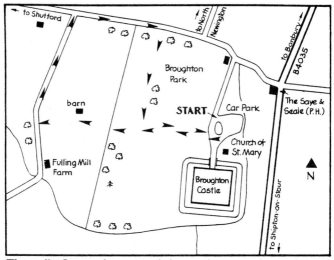

The walk: Leave the car park by passing over the cattle grid adjacent to the Church of St. Mary and you reach the main driveway to the house. Do not proceed to the gatehouse but bear right taking the grassy track up the hill directly in line with the church. Continue straight ahead to the top of the hill avoiding a feint cross-track. When you reach the top of the hill turn round to admire the beautiful undulating countryside and the superb views of Broughton Castle and the moat.

You now head left towards a small copse bounded by a wooden fence and soon reach a stile with a gate beside it. Pass through the gate and continue walking straight ahead along a footpath across a field which leads you to a barn. To the left of the barn is a stile with a public footpath sign marked with a yellow arrow. Climb over the stile and continue across another field keeping a hedge and fence to your right. At the other side of the field you reach another stile which you cross. Continue ahead along a track with Fulling Mill Farm on your left in the hollow. Proceed along the track with the wire fence on your right until you reach a gate. Pass through the gate and immediately turn right up the hill along a partly metalled lane until you reach a quiet single track road. At the road you turn right and once again you have good views of the surrounding rolling countryside. As you walk along the road keep to the right. You soon pass by a wooded area to your right. Then very shortly afterwards, before you reach another wooded area, you come to another stile on your right with a public footpath sign again marked with a yellow arrow.

Cross over the stile and proceed through some beech trees. You soon reach the top of the hill you climbed at the start of the walk and can enjoy once again excellent views of Broughton Castle. Walk down the slope to the car park where the walk began.

Historical Notes

H.N.1

Broughton Castle is open 18th May-14th September on Wednesdays and Sundays as well as on Thursdays in July and August. It is also open on Bank Holiday Sundays and Bank Holiday Mondays. The opening times are 2pm-5pm and the price of admission to the Castle and Gardens (not the parkland which is free) is £1.20 for adults and 70p for children. Parties can visit the house on other days throughout the year at reduced rates by appointment. Tel. Banbury (0295) 62624.

The original medieval Manor House, of which much still remains today, was built about 1300 by Sir John de Broughton who enlarged an existing building which lay within a large moat. In 1377 it was purchased by William of Wykeham and in 1451 it passed, by marriage, into the hands of the second Lord Saye and Sele in whose family it has since remained. The house was greatly enlarged between 1550 and 1600 and at this time it was embellished with superb plaster ceilings, splendid panelling and fine fireplaces. During the Civil War William, the eighth Lord Saye and Sele, was a distinguished leader of the Parliamentary forces. William opposed Charles I's efforts to rule without Parliament and Broughton became a secret meeting place for the king's enemies. When the War began William raised a regiment of blue-coats and four troops of horse. Together with his four sons he fought at the nearby Battle of Edgehill in 1642. After the battle the castle was besieged and captured. Many interesting relics of the Civil War are on show.

H.N.2

The unusual compound title of 'Saye and Sele' dates from the original creation of the barony in 1447. It is partly personal, from the connection with earlier 'Lords Say', and partly territorial through ownership of land in Kent. The present Lord Saye and Sele is the 21st baron.

H.N.3

The parish church of St. Mary dates almost entirely from the 14th century. On the south wall is an elaborate painted tomb of Sir John de Broughton and there is also a tomb of Sir Thomas Wykeham and his wife.

Blenheim Palace and Bladon

Introduction: Blenheim Palace (H.N.1), the exquisite home of the 11th Duke of Marlborough and birthplace of Sir Winston Churchill, forms the focal point of this superb family walk. You begin the walk near St. Martin's Church (H.N.2) in Bladon where Sir Winston Churchill is buried, before following a route through the Palace's magnificent park, across the famous Grand Bridge over the lake (H.N.3), and past the Palace itself. Moreover the walk takes you along a metalled road which is ideal for family walking at all times of the year.

In addition to the Palace itself all the family can enjoy a trip on the Blenheim lake in a motor launch, a ride on a miniature steam train, and a visit to the Garden Centre with its adjoining Walled Kitchen Garden.

Distance: Allow yourself about two hours to complete this 4½ mile circular walk. Naturally you will need more time if you wish to visit the Palace, take the boat trip, or enjoy the other facilities.

Refreshments: At the start of the walk by the side of the car park is the White House Pub which serves food and which has a beer garden. There is also a gift and refreshment centre in the northeast corner of the Palace which opens at 11am (Mondays at 11.30am) and closes at 6pm and is available to those not visiting the house. Visitors to the Palace can avail themselves of a wide variety of catering facilities. Luncheon is served from 12 noon-2pm and Afternoon Tea from 3.30pm in the Terrace Restaurant situated beside the Water Gardens. There is also a self-service Restaurant open from 11am-6pm.

How to get there: To reach the village of Bladon turn off the main A34 Oxford to Stratford-upon-Avon road onto the A4095 just south of Woodstock. Proceed along the road for about a mile and turn right at the White House Pub opposite Bladon Church of England Primary School. You can park in the car park adjacent to the pub for a small fee and limited free parking is available in the lane.

The walk: Proceed up the lane opposite Bladon Primary School and after about 150 yards you reach Bladon Lodge. You pass through the white kissing gate (after this point dogs must be kept on a lead) and continue up the metalled road past the swings and children's playground to your left. As you walk the south aspect of Blenheim Palace becomes visible to your left. After about 200 yards you turn left on a metalled road immediately in front of Middle Lodge.

Continue down the hill, cross the stone bridge and make your way up the hill on the other side. You pass through a wooded area

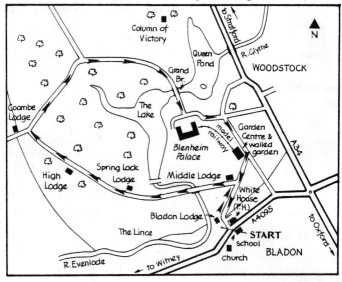

with fine views to your left. Soon you reach a small cottage on your right known as Spring Lock Lodge. Carry straight on through lovely woodland studded with oaks and after about half a mile you arrive at High Lodge on your left which is built beside two ponds. The path continues through the woods to Combe Lodge, but don't bear left towards the lodge: continue along the road which now curves to the right and downhill with woods on both sides. Proceed ahead an incline through beech woods and ignore the left hand fork in the road at the top of the hill.

After about five minutes walk you can see on your left the Column of Victory (H.N.4) at the entrance to the Great Avenue, and a few moments later you arrive at the Grand Bridge with the Palace directly in front of you. Cross over the Bridge and walk up the hill towards the Palace. Turn left in front of the House and walk past the gift shop to the visitors' entrance where you can begin your tour of this magnificent house with its superb treasures.

The walk continues along the main driveway for about 100 yards and turns right at a sign marked Garden Centre and Walled Garden. After 200 yards you will reach the model railway and shortly afterwards the Garden Centre. Soon the road forks and you turn right following a sign marked Bladon. After a few steps you reach Middle Lodge again and can then return to Bladon Lodge and the car park where the walk began.

Historical Notes

H.N.1
Blenheim Palace is open daily from 15th March to 31st October between 11.30am and 5.00pm (ticket office closes at 4.45pm). Tours of the palace are continuous at 5 to 10 minute intervals. Normally the tours are conducted but occasionally guides are positioned in rooms. The tour of the palace takes approximately one hour. The park is open daily from 9am to 5pm. For further information telephone Woodstock 812085 or 812112. Rides on the miniature steam railway which is run by the Witney and West Oxford Society of Model Engineers cost 15p. The railway operates at weekends during September and October.

The palace is the home of the 11th Duke of Marlborough and is the country's largest stately home. It was designed by Sir John Vanbrugh and was constructed between 1705 and 1722. It was the gift of Queen Anne to John Churchill, the 1st Duke of Marlborough, in honour of his victories in the War of Spanish Succession, and in particular in recognition of his defeat of the French and Bavarians at the Battle of Blenheim in 1704. The palace is a fine example of English Baroque architecture. Visitors to the palace can see the Great Hall with its magnificent ceiling painted by John Thornhill, the Three State Rooms, the beautiful Long Library, the room where Sir Winston Churchill was born on 30th November 1874, and a superb collection of furniture, paintings, sculpture and tapestries. There is also the Churchill Exhibition which includes some of Sir Winston Churchill's personal belongings, letters, books and photographs. It is also possible to stroll round the exquisite Water Gardens and admire the lovely fountains. The palace stands in over 2,000 acres of landscaped parkland.

For more detailed information we recommend that visitors purchase the excellent guidebook to the Palace.

H.N.2
The present Church of St. Martin, Bladon, dates from 1804 but a church existed on the site as far back as the 11th or 12th century. The graves of members of the Spencer-Churchill family are to be found on the north side of the Church Tower including those of Sir Winston Churchill (died 24th January 1965), his wife Clementine Ogilvy Spencer-Churchill (died 1977), his father Lord Randolph Spencer-Churchill (died 1895) and his mother Jennie Randolph Churchill (died 1921).

H.N.3
The Lake as we now know it was created in the 1760's by

Capability Brown who dammed the River Glyme. The Grand Bridge was designed earlier in the century by John Vanbrugh and its cost and immensity caused bitter disputes between Sarah Churchill, 1st Duchess of Marlborough, and the architect!

H.N.4
The Column of Victory was built between 1727 and 1730 at a cost of about £3,000. It is 134 feet high and the lead statue of the 1st Duke of Marlborough at the top of the column is the work of Robert Pit.

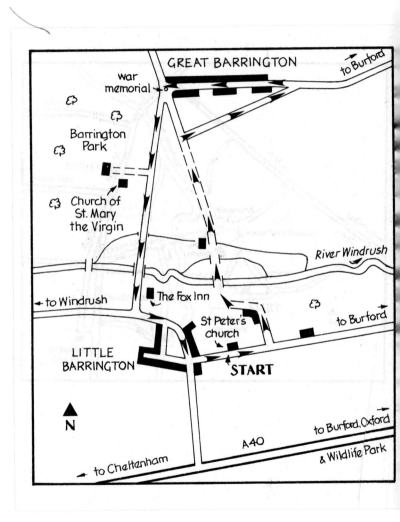

GREAT BARRINGTON

to Burford

war
memorial

Barrington
Park

Church of
St. Mary
the Virgin

River Windrush

to Windrush

The Fox Inn

St Peter's
church

to Burford

LITTLE
BARRINGTON

START

N

to Burford, Oxford

A40

& Wildlife Park

to Cheltenham

Great and Little Barrington and the Cotswold Wild Life Park

Introduction: This walk, on the Oxfordshire/Gloucestershire border, starts and finishes at St. Peter's Church (H.N.1) in the gorgeous village of Little Barrington, and also takes you to nearby Great Barrington on the other side of the River Windrush. The Barringtons are typical examples of tranquil, unspoilt Cotswold villages. After completing this short but delightful walk all the family may visit the Cotswold Wild Life Park (H.N.2) some five miles away. The Park is situated in beautifully wooded countryside and consists of 120 acres of gardens and parkland. It presents an interesting variety of mammals, birds, reptiles, fish, and insects from all over the world (including Zebras, Rhinos, Camels, Crocodiles, Rattlesnakes, Leopards, Tigers, Giant Spiders, Otters, Monkeys, Penguins and Pelicans) living under almost natural conditions. You can picnic on the spacious lawns and watch your children enjoying themselves in the adventure playground, or stroll beneath the trees for which the Park is famous. Other attractions include Pet's Corner, a Narrow Gauge Railway, Donkey and Pony Rides, a Garden Centre, Landscaped Gardens, an Animal Brass Rubbing Centre, and a Conservation Display.

Distance: The walk, which is very easy, is 1½ miles in length and should take no more than an hour to complete.

Refreshments: The Fox Inn on the road between Great and Little Barrington has a small beer garden on the banks of the River Windrush and serves good snacks. In the Wild Life Park there is a Restaurant/Self-Service Cafeteria which is open daily for meals

17

and snacks. It is situated at the rear of the Manor House and seats 250 people. The service is reduced in winter. The restaurant also has a bar which is open from 10am to 2.30pm. In addition the Park has refreshment kiosks situated near the Zebra House, the Walled Garden, and in Pet's Corner and near the Adventure Playground.

How to get there: Little Barrington is situated just off the A40, approximately three miles west of Burford. After leaving the A40 proceed to Little Barrington where you take the first right up a small incline to the church. Park near the church.

The Wild Life Park is about two miles south of Burford on the A361 Burford/Swindon road and is well signposted.

The walk: Little Barrington Church is quite delightful and worth visiting. Turn left out of the churchyard and walk down the road for about 100 yards until you come to a junction where you turn left. Continue down the hill and follow the road which curves to the left. At the bottom of the hill you will see a Public Footpath sign. Follow the sign to the right crossing a bridge over the River Windrush and passing through a gate. You are now in the beautiful river valley. Follow the track straight ahead for about 200 yards keeping a wire fence to your left (after rain this short section of the walk may be muddy under foot). At the far end of the track you reach a gate and a bridge which you cross, and then proceed for a short distance until you reach a stone house.

Walk in front of the house and continue along a track up the hill. At the top of the hill bear right along a lane noticing the charming views along the Windrush Valley to your right. You pass some derelict houses before the lane curves round to the left to reach the main road. Turn left and for the next 50 yards or so proceed with care until you join the footpath on the right which takes you through the pleasant village of Great Barrington. You pass by some stone houses in the village and quickly come to the War Memorial. Here you turn left down the hill following the sign post to Little Barrington. The footpath on the right-hand side of the road skirts a high stone wall and after a few paces you pass the entrance to Barrington Park (not open to the public). Immediately past this entrance on the right you follow a metalled path to the Church of St. Mary the Virgin, Great Barrington (H.N.3).

When you have visited the church continue down the hill and cross the bridge over the River Windrush. Now take the footpath to your left and follow the road whilst enjoying the views across the fields towards Little Barrington Church where the walk began. Very soon you pass over another bridge and arrive at the Fox Inn on the left. Only a few steps past the pub you come to a junction where you bear left in the direction signposted Little Barrington. The meandering River Windrush can be seen to your left. When you come to the village you may wish to take a stroll to admire its quaint Cotswold stone cottages set behind a large grassy hollow. After this, turn left by the telephone kiosk up the lane to the point where the walk began.

Historical Notes

H.N.1
St. Peter's Church, Little Barrington, dates back to Norman times. Together with the church in neighbouring Windrush it was originally a dependent chapel of the Church at Great Barrington which was dedicated in 1159 by Alfred, Bishop of Worcester. The tower was built in the 12th century and two additional storeys were added in the 15th century. An interesting little booklet outlining the church's history is available inside the church. Amongst the church's interesting features is a small group of four stone figures in bold relief situated on the east side of the porch. It is a monument to William Tayler 1699, but the four figures appear to be much older than the inscription, although their origin remains obscure.

H.N.2
The Cotswold Wild Life Park is open daily throughout the year (except Christmas Day) from 10am to 6pm, or dusk (whichever is the earlier). Admission prices: Adults £1.70, children over three and Old Age Pensioners 90p. Enquiries to: Cotswold Wild Life

Park Office, Burford, Oxfordshire, Tel. Burford (099382) 3006 (office hours) and Restaurant (099382) 2005. Dogs are permitted in the Park provided they are kept on a lead. No dogs are allowed in any of the Walk-Through enclosures.

The Gothic style Manor House was built in 1804 to replace a previous Jacobean residence. The house and park formed the centre of the large Bradwell Grove Estate. The official guidebook to the Park tells us that here "for many centuries farming and forestry has combined to form a typical example of Cotswold life. The owner, John Heyworth, inherited the estate from his grandfather, Colonel Heyworth Savage in 1949 and twenty years later decided to open the Park to the public."

H.N.3

The church has been much restored and altered at different periods. It was originally a Norman building. Two interesting features of the church are: firstly in the churchyard against a wall, an old long stone seat with "elbows" which may well have originally been placed inside the church; and secondly an effigy in the North Aisle of Captain Edmund Bray (d. 1620) in Tudor armour. It appears that when Queen Elizabeth I forgave Edmund Bray for killing a man Bray swore he would never use his right hand on his sword again. You will notice that the sword is on the left-hand side of his tomb.

The church stands adjacent to Barrington Park with its great deer park and its late Renaissance style mansion built by Charles Talbot, who was Lord Chancellor in the reign of George II.

Witney and the Manor Farm Museum, Cogges

Introduction: This combination of family outing and interesting walk is centred on the Manor Farm Museum at Cogges (H.N.1), a small hamlet just a short stroll from Witney. You will be able to enjoy: the Edwardian museum with its farm animals, its dairy, its farmhouse showing the work of the household, its farmyard displays illustrating the seasonal activities on the farm, its picnic area in the orchard, its Historical Trail around the farm buildings, the moated manor and archaeological remains, and its Nature Trail through the farm and meadows by the banks of the River Windrush. The walk itself takes you through the centre of Witney (H.N.2) with its famous 17th century Buttercross and its fine Church Green surrounded by the imposing Church of St. Mary (H.N.3), and buildings of architectural distinction.

Distance: The route chosen is about 2¼ miles in length and will only take about an hour to complete. Clearly you should allow considerably longer if you wish to visit the museum and take the Historical and Nature Trails.

Refreshments: The museum contains a refreshment bar in one of the converted stock sheds and a selection of pubs and cafes can be found in Witney.

How to get there: By car from the centre of Witney take the B4022 road towards Oxford and follow the signs to the Farm Museum Car Park.

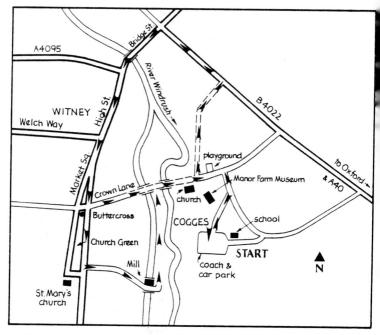

The walk: From the car park follow the signs to the entrance to the museum. After visiting the museum turn left and follow a public footpath sign marked Town Centre. At the end of the lane turn left again. You pass a small children's playground on your right and continue ahead keeping Cogges Parish Church (H.N.4) and the museum buildings to your left. After about 50 yards you turn right through a kissing gate and follow the path leading over a wooden bridge. The River Windrush can be seen away to your left. Keep straight on along the path and at the far end of the field you go through a gate before proceeding along a narrow path with a wire fence to your right. You soon reach the main road (the B4022) where you turn left. There is a pleasant row of Cotswold stone houses on your left and shortly afterwards on your right you reach some almshouses (H.N.5).

At the road junction turn left into Bridge Street following the sign to Bampton. After about 200 yards you come to the bridge over the River Windrush where you may wish to pause awhile to look down river. Immediately past the bridge turn left along the High Street past the Methodist Church on the left, and Welch Way on your right. You soon come to the Post Office on your right. Just a few yards past the Post Office bear left and after a short distance you arrive at the Buttercross where Witney's market was traditionally held. At this point you may wish to shorten the walk by turning left along Crown Lane Footpath which quickly brings you back to the museum.

However, if you wish to walk over the delightful Church Green and visit the Parish Church of St. Mary the Virgin, continue ahead. After visiting the church turn right outside the church gates, cross over the road and proceed down Farm Mill Lane. You soon leave the busy streets of Witney behind you as the lane turns into a rough track. Carry on along this track and after about 200 yards you cross a bridge over a small stream. Shortly afterwards you bear left and you reach a mill on your left and immediately walk over a bridge directly in front of the mill. Turn sharp left and cross over a stile. Continue straight ahead across the field (which may be muddy after rain) to another stile over which you climb. Very soon you will see two white bridges one to your left and the other to your right. You take the bridge to your right and the lane leads you back to Cogges, the museum and the car park.

Historical Notes

H.N.1

Manor Farm Museum is open from 1st May to the end of October, from 11am to 6pm daily. The admission price is: adults 80p and children over five years and OAPs 25p. The farmyard displays include implements and machinery used on the farm in the 19th century such as carts and wagons, dairy equipment, and ploughs. At the weekends there are demonstrations of old farm skills including cream and butter making, blacksmithing, hurdlemaking, threshing, and bridlemaking.

The Manor of Cogges was settled as early as 1086 when the hamlet is mentioned in the Domesday Book. The first manor house was situated by the side of the River Windrush and in the

13th century the de Grey family built a new house on higher ground. During the 16th and 17th centuries significant alterations were made to the house and a new wing was added on the east side. Since then the external appearance of the house has hardly changed.

H.N.2

Witney is, of course, famous for its blankets which have been produced in the town for at least 700 years. The town made use of the two traditional sources of wealth in the Cotswolds: fleece and fast flowing water. A monument to the woollen industry is the Blanket Hall built in 1721 at the junction of the High Street and Mill Street. Here blankets were brought for weighing and measuring before they were dispatched. Blankets can still be bought in the town.

During the medieval period Witney was a busy market town. The market was held around the Buttercross with its 13 pillars which stands opposite the Market Hall. The Bishop of Winchester owned a residence in the town and both Henry II and King John often visited Witney. It is believed that it was at Witney that John summoned a parliament to Oxford to discuss the Magna Carta.

H.N.3

The official booklet outlining the history of Witney Parish Church of St. Mary the Virgin states: "the church has been described as one of the most striking and interesting edifices in the Diocese of Oxford and indeed even the most casual visitor could hardly fail to be impressed by the first sight of the imposing building as seen from the Green". It is thought that a Saxon church probably stood on the site and certainly a church of considerable size was built on this spot after the Norman Conquest. However, all that remains of the Norman Church is the porch, the central portion of the walls of the nave, and a few finely carved stones built into the walls. The rest of the present church is principally Early English. Among the most notable features of the building are the fine Early English tower, the magnificent 150 foot spire, the Wenman Tomb and Chapel, and the decorated window in the North Transept which is perhaps the finest such window in the county. The church registers are well preserved and date back to 1559.

H.N.4
A simple and small church was established in the 11th century and since then there have been several additions to the original structure. For example, new aisles were added in the 12th century and in the 13th century the chancel was rebuilt and enlarged. A most unusual feature of the church was a crypt which underlay the eastern half of the chancel. The crypt has now been destroyed. In the 14th century the North Chapel was added and it may have been a chantry served from the priory. The north aisle was rebuilt shortly afterwards with a peculiarly positioned angle tower. The monks probably used the aisle for their own services. Other interesting features of the church include a Norman tub-shaped font, a memorial to the Blake family, and an effigy of Isabella de Grey which dates from the mid-14th century.

H.N.5
A weather-worn plaque on the front of the building states: "These almshouses were built and endowed by William Townsend a native of this town and haberdasher of Holborn, London, for the use of aged unmarried women. 1821".

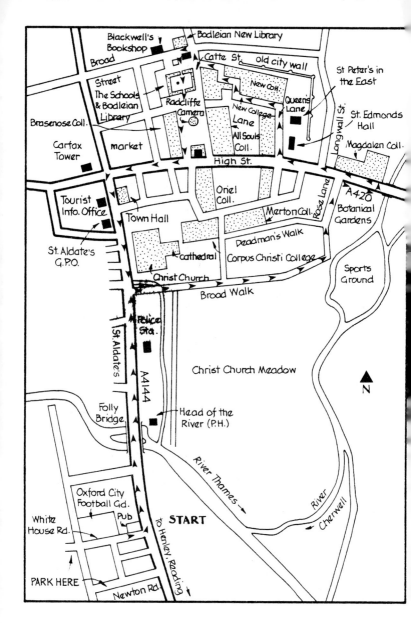

START

N

26

WALK FIVE

Oxford, Christ Church Meadow, the Botanic Garden and "The High"

Introduction: The city of Oxford is internationally famous for its University colleges and its magnificent buildings and museums. This walk is not intended to be a historical tour of Oxford but it is hoped that in a small way it will help the family to capture something of the atmosphere of this fascinating city. The circuit covers just a small part of central Oxford and takes in the Broad Walk by the side of Christ Church Meadow, several important colleges (including Christ Church, Magdalen and New College), the Botanic Garden, the famous High Street, the Examination Schools, the Sheldonian Theatre, the Bodleian Library and Carfax Tower.

After completing the walk you may wish to visit other of the colleges or perhaps the Ashmolean Museum of Art and Archaeology or the Museum of the History of Science. In summer some may wish to take a boat ride down the Thames to Abingdon whilst the more adventurous may want to try their hand at punting on the River Cherwell. In any event visitors are strongly recommended to contact the Tourist Information Centre (Tel. Oxford 726871/2 or 249811) in St. Aldates (opposite the Town Hall) in order to discover full details about what the city has to offer. For those interested in Oxford's history many detailed historical guides are available.

Distance: The walk itself is a circuit of approximately two miles and should only take about an hour to complete. But in addition you will probably wish to spend time visiting the Botanic Garden and the various colleges and places referred to below.

Refreshments: Near the start of the walk on the Oxford side of Folly Bridge is the Head of the River pub which has an outside terrace by the side of the Thames together with Bumpers Tea Shop. About mid-way through the walk on the corner of the High Street and Queen's Lane is the Queen's Lane Coffee House. In addition there are numerous pubs, snack bars and restaurants in the city centre.

How to get there: The walk begins just south of the city centre and you should park off the Abingdon Road (the A4144) either in the Free Overflow Car Park in Newton Road which is open between April and September (opposite Queen's College Cricket Ground). Alternatively you may park in Whitehouse Road (again just off the Abingdon Road) by the side of Oxford City Football Club. Parking here is limited to three hours between Monday and Saturday 8am to 6.30pm. You may also park in any of the city centre car parks and then make your way to Folly Bridge.

The walk: Assuming you have parked in either the Newton Road Overflow Car Park or in Whitehouse Road, make your way back to Abingdon Road and turn left. Pass by Oxford City Football Ground and continue over Folly Bridge (H.N.1). Just before the bridge on the right is the office of Salter Brothers Passenger Boats Co. where you can arrange to take boat trips along the Thames. As you cross over Folly Bridge look right and in the distance on the Oxford side of the river you will see the University Boathouses (H.N.2) which provide a grandstand finish to the rowing events in Eights Week.

Immediately after crossing Folly Bridge you come to the Head of the River pub. Carry on straight ahead along St. Aldates past the Police Station and the University of Oxford Faculty of Music on the right until you arrive at the entrance to Christ Church Meadow (H.N.3) also on your right (directly opposite the Restaurant Elizabeth). Pass through the wrought iron gateway and after a few paces you will see the War Memorial Garden on your left. Carry straight on and after about 100 yards you reach the public entrance to Christ Church (H.N.4) on your left. Tom

Quad, the Cathedral and the Hall are all essential viewing. Return to the point where you entered Christ Church after you have completed your visit and turn left. You are soon walking along the delightful Broad Walk (H.N.5). In the distance to your left you can see Magdalen Tower, and the playing fields which you pass by on your left belong to Merton College and are known as Merton Fields. At the end of Broad Walk turn round and pause awhile to enjoy a good view of part of Oxford's beautiful skyline of "Dreaming Spires".

Now proceed until you reach the River Cherwell with Magdalen College School Sports Ground on the opposite bank away to your right. At the river turn left through an avenue of trees until you come to the exit gate from the Meadow. Go through the gate into Rose Lane and after about 200 yards turn right passing in front of a rose garden and walk on to the entrance to the remarkable Botanic Garden (H.N.6).

When you have completed your visit to the garden go straight ahead up some steps which lead on to the famous "High". The glorious 144 feet tall Magdalen Tower is now directly in front of you and Magdalen Bridge is on your right (punts may be hired on the Cherwell from below the bridge). Cross over the "High" and turn left. After a few yards you come to the entrance to Magdalen College (H.N.7) on your right. Here you may visit the Hall, the Chapel and Cloisters, the Deer Park and take Addison's Walk through the Water Meadows.

After completing your visit to Magdalen College turn right down the "High", go past Longwall Street to the right and Merton Street and the imposing buildings of the Examination Schools (H.N.8) to the left. Shortly you come to Queen's Lane on the right. You follow this lane which winds its way past St. Edmund Hall and the church of St. Peter in-the-East both of which are on your right, and one of the perimeter walls of Queen's College to your left. After about 200 yards Queen's Lane becomes New College Lane and you pass under an archway and then turn right to pay a visit to New College (II.N.9) with its impressive Quadrangle, Cloister, Chapel, Hall and beautiful gardens which are flanked on two sides by the old city wall.

On finishing your tour of New College and its grounds continue along New College Lane bearing right then left under the exquisite Bridge of Sighs (built 1903) which connects two parts of Hertford College. You are now in Catte Street. Turn right, then sharp left into Broad Street where you can see the New Bodleian Library and the internationally known Blackwell's Bookshop to your right, and on your left the "Emperors' Heads" outside the Sheldonian Theatre (H.N.10) which is open to the public and well worth visiting. Proceed up the steps in front of the Sheldonian Theatre and bear left towards an archway and a pair of wrought iron gates. Pass through the archway and you enter the Old School's Quadrangle with its bronze statue by Hubert le Sueur of William Herbert, third Earl of Pembroke. The entrance to the Bodleian Library (H.N.11) is on your right and you may visit a small part of the library and look at the exhibition pieces.

Turn right outside the library entrance and pass through a second archway, similar to the first one you encountered, and you are now in Radcliffe Square which is dominated by the Radcliffe Camera (H.N.12). It should be noted that if you arrive at the Sheldonian Theatre at a time when it is closed and the archways referred to above are not open to the public you will have to enter Radcliffe Square from Catte Street. Walk by the side of Radcliffe Camera and bear right past the entrance to Brasenose College. Shortly you rejoin the High Street with St. Mary's Church on your left which incorporates a brass rubbing centre.

At this point you turn sharp right and continue along the "High" past the Covered Market until you reach St. Martin's Tower, Carfax (H.N.13). Here you turn left at the crossroads in front of the Tower down St. Aldates passing the Tourist Information Centre on your right, and the Town Hall and the Museum of Oxford on your left. Continue down St. Aldates past the magnificent buildings of Christ Church and Tom Tower, over Folly Bridge and back to the start of the walk.

Historical Notes

H.N.1

There has been a bridge on this site for centuries. Certainly a bridge existed here in 1220 and until 1779 halfway across the bridge there stood a tower and gateway which may have been, at one time, part of the city's defences. The tower was apparently a vantage point from which Roger Bacon (ca. 1214-94) studied astronomy. The tower was known as Bachelor's Tower, Friar Bacon's Study and the Folly from which the bridge took its name.

H.N.2

Inter-college eight-oared races first took place in 1815 when Brasenose were Head of the River, and Jesus College was possibly their only competitor. During the 19th century, Eights Week at the end of May each year developed into one of the major occasions of the Oxford sporting and social calendar. The principle of the races has always been that boats start one behind another in a single line, with a uniform distance between each boat, and each tries to bump the one in front. The college whose boat is first over the finishing line in the final race having not been bumped is pronounced Head of the River for that year. In 1874 the large number of boats entering made it necessary to row the races in divisions for the first time and this is still the case today.

H.N.3

Christ Church Meadow is open every day from 7am to dusk. No dogs allowed. Lady Montacute (d. 1354) gave part of the land which is now the Meadow to maintain her Chantry in the Lady Chapel at the Priory of St. Frideswide (now Christ Church Cathedral). Her tomb can be found in the Cathedral. On 3rd April 1524 Cardinal Wolsey obtained a Bull from Pope Clement to dissolve St. Frideswide's Priory and the Meadow together with the Priory and its other possessions became part of Wolsey's short-lived Cardinal College which subsequently was re-established as Christ Church College. The Meadow is held in trust by Christ Church as green countryside and is still grazed by cattle. In 1965 plans to build a road through the Meadow were staunchly and successfully opposed.

H.N.4

A good time to visit Christ Church with Tom Quad, the Chapter House, Cathedral and Hall, which is one of the finest in the country, is between 10am and 12.30pm or between 2pm and 4pm. The admission prices are: Adults 50p and Old Age Pensioners, Students and Children (10-16 years old) 15p. If one of the following — Chapter House, Cathedral, Hall — is closed then admission for adults is 40p, and if two of the above are closed then admission is free.

Christ Church Picture Gallery is open Mondays to Saturdays 10.30am-1pm and 2pm-4.30pm. The admission price is 30p (free on Thursdays). Entrance is by Canterbury Gate via Blue Boar Street, Bear Lane and Oriel Square.

The College was founded in 1525 by Cardinal Wolsey and was originally known as Cardinal College. After Wolsey's fall the College was refounded in 1532 by Henry VIII under the name of King Henry VIII's College, and again in 1545 when it was given the present name and the College was united with the newly established See of Oxford. It then became a cathedral and college in one, an arrangement which has survived until today. The splendid Tom Tower was completed by Sir Christoper Wren in 1682. Great Tom, the bell situated in the Tower, tolls 101 times every evening at 9.05pm. This was the sign for closing the College gates until the early 20th century and the 101 strokes stems from the fact that there were originally 101 students at the College. Features include the Canterbury Quad, Peckwater Quad, Tom Quad, the Hall, the Cathedral, the 15th century Refectory, the Chapter House and the Picture Gallery which was opened in 1968 and contains 300 paintings and 1,700 drawings dating from the period 1300-1750.

The College has produced 13 Prime Ministers including Peel, Gladstone, and Salisbury. Other famous students include Sir Philip Sidney, John Locke, William Penn, John Wesley, C.L. Dodgson (Lewis Carroll), and W.H. Auden.

H.N.5

Broad Walk is reputed to have been constructed from the material excavated during the building of Cardinal College. Up until 1976 there was a splendid avenue of Elms along Broad Walk which had originally been planted by Dean Fell in 1668. The Elms were felled because they had been afflicted by Elm disease. The walk has now been replanted with Oriental and hybrid Plane trees.

H.N.6

The opening times of the Botanic Garden are: March-October (British Summer Time) weekdays 8.30am-5.30pm, Sundays 10am-12am and 2pm-6pm; October-March (Greenwich Mean Time) weekdays 9am-4.30pm, Sundays 10am-12am and 2pm-4pm. The Greenhouses are open daily between 2pm and 4pm. Children are admitted only in the care of adults. No dogs or cycles allowed. No radios or cassette players and no picking of plants, flowers or seeds.

The Garden was founded in 1621 by the Earl of Danby and is the oldest of its kind in Britain. It was originally intended for the culture of medical plants but today plants are grown in the open and under glass for teaching and research in botany and allied subjects. The gateway to the Garden was designed by the sculptor Nicholas Stone and incorporates statues of Charles I and Charles II and a bust of the Earl of Danby.

The first and probably the most famous plant to "escape" from the Garden was the Oxford Ragwort which was originally introduced from Sicily where it grows on volcanic terrain. By the end of the 18th century the Oxford Ragwort was recorded as growing on old walls in Oxford and over the next two centuries it became widely distributed throughout England and Wales. The plant was spread in part by the railways and the Ragwort thrived along cindered railway cuttings in conditions similar to those in its native Sicily.

H.N.7

Magdalen (pronounced Maudlin) College is open to visitors between 2pm and 6.15pm daily. All rooms and staircases are strictly private. For the Deer Park and walks go through the Cloisters. All Chapel services are open to the public. No dogs,

33

transistor radios, bicycles. Be as quiet as possible.

The College was founded in 1458 by William of Waynflete (d. 1486). The Tower, attributed to Wolsey, was begun in 1492 and finished in 1509. On the morning of 1st May the choir sing from the top of the Tower. Other main features are the Chapel, the Hall, the Library, the State Rooms, the Cloisters and the New Buildings. Amongst the famous men who studied at Magdalen were Cardinal Wolsey, John Hampden, Edward Gibbon and Oscar Wilde.

H.N.8

The Examination Schools are no longer open to the public. The architect of the Schools was Sir T.G. Jackson, R.A. and the building was opened in 1882. The marble pillars, mosaic pavement and grand staircase inside the building are particularly noteworthy. At the beginning of June, Oxford students take their examinations here but during the rest of the year the rooms are used for lectures, conferences and other educational activities.

H.N.9

New College is open to visitors during term time between 2pm and 6pm and during the vacation between 11am and 6pm. No dogs. Please keep off the grass. The places open to visitors are the Cloisters, the Chapel, the Hall and the Gardens. Founded in 1379 by William of Wykeham, the College has the oldest quadrangle in Oxford. One of the wardens of the College was W.A. Spooner who invented the Spoonerism. Famous men associated with the College include: John Galsworthy, Sidney Smith, Sir A.P. Herbert and George Woodcock.

H.N.10

The Sheldonian Theatre is generally open to visitors, except between 1pm and 2pm each weekday as follows: 15th February to 15th November 10am to 5pm and 16th November to 14th February 10am to 4pm. It is not open on public holidays and other days when it is in use for ceremonies, meetings or concerts. Admission prices: adults 15p and school children 5p.

The Sheldonian Theatre was built between 1664 and 1669 to accommodate important university functions and particularly the ceremony at the end of the summer term known as Encaenia when honorary degrees are awarded and benefactors commemorated. It was formally given to the university in 1669 by Gilbert Sheldon, Archbishop of Canterbury. It was the first large commission undertaken by Christopher Wren. Wren's roof was rebuilt in 1803 and the building was restored between 1959 and 1960. The theatre has an outstanding painted ceiling, the work of Robert Streater, the Serjeant Painter to Charles II. There is a good view of the spires of Oxford from the cupola.

H.N.11

The Bodleian Library is open Monday to Friday between 9am and 5pm, and Saturday between 9am and 12.30pm. Only a restricted area is open to visitors, and this includes the Divinity School and the Exhibition Rooms which display some of the library's treasures. The library was originally founded by Humphrey, Duke of Gloucester in ca. 1445. The earliest part of the library is the absolutely magnificent 'Duke Humphrey' with its elaborate ceiling, which was finished in 1490. The library was refounded by Thomas Bodley between 1598 and 1602 after the books had been dispersed during the reign of Edward VI. As a Copyright Library the Bodleian is entitled to receive a copy of every new work published within the United Kingdom. The library now has over two million volumes. The Radcliffe Camera and the New Bodleian are linked to the Old Library by underground tunnels.

H.N.12

The Radcliffe Camera is probably the finest example of a circular library in England. Dr. John Radcliffe, the physician to William III and his Queen, Queen Anne and Prince George of Denmark, left £40,000 for the construction of a library. After some twenty years of negotiation the land was eventually freed for building purposes and work began in 1737. The library, which was designed by James Gibbs, was finished in 1748 and opened in 1749. In 1803 the lower arches were glazed and a new entrance constructed to make available an additional reading room. Originally intended as a Science library, the Radcliffe Camera has for many years been a general reading room of the Bodleian Library.

H.N.13

Carfax Tower is open in the summer only between 10.30am and 12.30pm and 2.30pm and 4.30pm on weekdays and Saturdays, and on Sundays between 2pm and 5pm. Visitors can obtain an excellent view of Oxford from the top of the Tower. Carfax Tower is all that remains of the medieval Church of St. Martin which stood on this site until 1819. The medieval church was demolished in that year to make way for a new church which was constructed between 1820 and 1822. This church was in turn demolished in 1896 as a result of the Oxford Corporation Act of 1890 which provided for the removal of the church on the grounds that its presence made the streets of Oxford too narrow for the increased traffic. However, the tower was again saved and today represents a central landmark and meeting place.

Abingdon and the Abbey Grounds

Introduction: This walk is an ideal afternoon stroll and is suitable even for young children. There are plenty of facilities en route which cater for the needs of the family, including a swimming pool, a paddling pool, a crazy golf course, and the Abbey Park and grounds. There is also an opportunity to visit some of the older parts of Abingdon as well as Abingdon Abbey, the Long Gallery and the Checker. The walk also has excellent views along the Thames.

Make sure of appropriate footwear since the path alongside the river may be muddy under foot in some places after a rainy spell. And if you intend to complete the entire walk, which involves crossing Abingdon lock, consult the table below to check when the walkway across the lock is open to the public. The walkway is quite suitable for children who are properly supervised, but walkers crossing the lock do so at their own risk and although the Thames Water Authority allow the public to use the path over the weir it is not a public right of way.

Month	Times when open to public
JAN-MAR	0900-16.15
APR	0900-17.30
MAY	0900-18.30
JUN-AUG	0900-19.00
SEPT	0900-18.00
OCT	0900-17.00
NOV-DEC	0900-16.15

N.B. Wednesdays May-Oct. Walkway opens at 0930

Distance: About 1¾ miles and should take about 1½ hours to complete. Allow longer if you wish to visit the Abbey Museum or stroll around the Abbey Grounds and along the river.

Refreshments: There are numerous good Public Houses and some cafes in Abingdon, many of which you will pass during the course of the walk. Suggestions include The Abingdon Bridge Restaurant and Trotman's Cafe in Ock Street. An excellent pub with a wide range of food and a beer garden is The Ox, which is a little way out of the centre on the Oxford Road past the area known as the Vineyard.

How to get there: By car when arriving in the centre of Abingdon follow the one way system along Stert Street and take the Henley and Culham Road and the large Car Park (Rye Farm Vehicle Park) is on your left just across the bridge over the Thames.

The walk: Turn right after leaving the car park and cross over Abingdon Bridge keeping to the pavement on the right. As you cross the bridge there are fine views of the River Thames to left

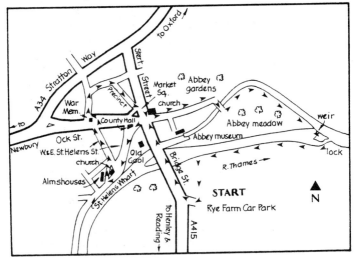

and right and there is also a good view to your left of St. Helen's Church Spire. Passing the Nags Head Public House proceed along Bridge Street with the Napoleonic prison now encompassing the Old Gaol Leisure and Community Centre on your left until you reach the Market Square with its impressive 17th century County Hall (H.N.1). Turn left crossing over Bridge Street, and keeping to the left of County Hall, continue down East St. Helen's Street with its beautiful Georgian houses and the Kings Head and Bell Public House which was formerly one of Abingdon's famous coaching Inns and where Charles I held some of his Councils of War during the English Civil War. At the end of East St. Helen's Street pass to the left of St. Helen's church and you quickly reach St. Helen's Wharf. To your left there is an excellent view of Abingdon Bridge which you crossed at the start of the walk. Stroll along the Wharf for about 100 yards and turn right through a gate with a lamp above it, just before the Old Anchor Public House. You are now in Long Alley with the 15th century Christ's Hospital Almshouses on your left (H.N.2). At the end of Long Alley turn right passing by the side of St. Helen's Church. You proceed through an archway and the entrance to this beautiful Church (well worth visiting H.N.3) is on your right. Turn left on to West St. Helen's Street. At the top of West St. Helen's Street turn right along High Street and almost immediately cross over High Street at the pelican crossing. Again turn left and walk along High Street past the Post Office to The Square with its War Memorial. At this point you turn right into Bath Street. Continue along Bath Street for about 200 yards and you reach the Black Swan Public House where you turn right and right again into the Bury Street Shopping Precinct. Continue through the precinct until you reach the Market Square again where you bear left and pass through an archway by the side of Menzies Shop. You are now on Stert Street. Cross over Stert Street at the pedestrian crossing and turn right. You soon arrive at St. Nicholas' Church (H.N.4) where you turn left and pass under The Abbey Gateway (with its amusing gargoyles).

Those wishing to visit the Checker and Long Gallery (the remaining parts of the Old Abbey Buildings H.N.5) continue along the road and turn right into Checker Way. You then follow the arrows to The Abbey Museum entrance.

For those continuing the walk through the Abbey Grounds you turn left through a gate into Abbey House and Grounds.

As you walk along note the beautiful sequoia trees. You proceed down a set of steps and follow the path by the side of the wall. You can see what appears to be some of the Abbey ruins on your right as you walk along this path. These are, in fact, an architectural fantasy built during the 19th century by E.J. Trendell and known as Trendell's Folly.

Just before you reach the children's playground you go through a gate on the right. You cross over a bridge and this will bring you into the Park (there are a number of amenities here including a paddling pool, swimming pool, crazy golf course and tennis courts).

Once you have crossed over the bridge you turn left immediately and follow a track alongside a small river which, after about half a mile, brings you to the weir and lock. Cross over with care. (If the gates to the walkway are locked you will have to return to the Market Square through the park grounds). At the other side of the lock turn right and continue along the path by the side of the river. Just before the bridge turn left and cross a field to a stile which brings you back to the car park and the start of the walk.

Historical Notes

H.N.1

The Market Square, or Bury, and County Hall (formerly called the Market Hall) form the distinctive focal point of Abingdon, which is now the administrative centre for the Vale of the White Horse District and which used to be the County town of Royal Berkshire.

A market has been held in the Bury for some eight centuries and there has been a Market House on the site of the present County Hall since before 1327. Building work on County Hall, a handsome ashlar and stone renaissance building was started in

1678 and completed in 1683. It is probably the work of Christopher Kempster, from Burford. Kempster was one of the master masons engaged by Sir Christopher Wren for the rebuilding of St. Paul's Cathedral and some believe that Wren himself may have provided the design for Abingdon although other observers see the hand of Inigo Jones in the building's architecture. The structure, which originally cost £2,840 to build, was restored for the first time in 1857 and between 1952 and 1956 the Ministry of Works, which considered the building one of the finest Stuart Civic Buildings in England, also organised extensive restoration work. The Square used to be much larger, extending down East St. Helen's Street to Lombard Street and along High Street to its junction with West St. Helen's Street, as well as taking up a larger area on its eastern side. The stocks, whipping post, pillory and cage as well as a Maypole used to be situated here in addition to the statue of Queen Victoria. The latter can now be seen in the Abbey Grounds.

H.N.2

A plaque in front of the almshouses, describes their history as follows: "The medieval fraternity of the Holy Cross was incorporated in 1441 by a royal charter and built the Long Alley Almshouses in 1446-47. The fraternity came to an end a century later as part of the Reformation but another royal charter of 1553, obtained largely through the influence of a famous Abingdonian, Sir John Mason, created the body known as Christ's Hospital which has been responsible since then for the administration of the Almshouses. Between 1605 and 1618 the outside porches and the lantern were added and the hall was panelled and furnished. The other Almshouses, Brick Alley to the south and Twitty's to the north, were built by Christ's Hospital early in the 18th century."

H.N.3

St. Helen's Church, which has five aisles, is said to be one of two Churches in England with a greater width than length. It dates principally from the 13th century and its spire was rebuilt in 1662.

The roof of the Lady Chapel dates from the 14th century and displays a rare medieval painting which represents the Tree of Jesse.

H.N.4

Sometimes known as the "Little Church in the Gate" St. Nicholas' Church still retains its original Norman doorway, some 13th century lancets, an unusual stone lantern with smoke funnel and a Jacobean pulpit. It dates from the 12th century and was built for Abingdon Abbey's servants and tenants. The Abbey-Gateway dates from the 15th century and between ca. 1860-65 the gateway was used as a Police Station.

H.N.5

Visitors to the Abbey Museum can obtain tickets from the Curator's Office. The museum is open 2pm-6pm, weekdays and Sundays throughout the year. Admission prices are: adults 20p and children (7-14 years old) 10p. Abingdon Abbey was founded in the 7th century. It was twice sacked by the Danes and rebuilt in the 10th century. The Abbey developed into one of the greatest Benedictine Houses in England and became a major ecclesiastical institution. William the Conqueror spent Easter at the Abbey in 1084 and left his youngest son, later King Henry I, to be educated by the monks here. At the time of the Domesday Survey the Abbey was the largest landowner in Berkshire after the King. The Abbey dominated the life of Abingdon until the Dissolution of the Monasteries at the time of the Reformation. It surrendered to Henry VIII on 8th February 1538.

The Abbey site was much more extensive than it is today stretching from Abingdon Bridge, to Stert Street, to the area known as The Vineyard, and to Abingdon Lock.

Long Wittenham, Appleford and The Pendon Museum

Introduction: This pleasant family walk begins in Long Wittenham (south of Abingdon), a charming and tranquil village on either side of a long street, and takes you to Appleford Church and along the banks of the Thames. It also passes the Pendon Museum. This village museum contains realistic and historically accurate miniature village and landscape scenes incorporating model railway systems. See H.N.3 for times of opening.

Distance: The circuit is about three miles and should take about 1½ hours to complete. Allow longer if you plan to visit the museum and the churches at Long Wittenham and Appleford.

Refreshments: There are three pubs in Long Wittenham. The Plough is particularly recommended for it serves good bar meals, has a large beer garden, and offers a leisurely stroll down to the Thames. Also at nearby Clifton Hampden is the famous Barley Mow public house where Jerome K. Jerome stayed while writing *Three Men in a Boat*. The Barley Mow allows children in one of its rooms and also has a beer garden.

How to get there: Turn off the A415 Abingdon to Henley Road at Clifton Hampden about four miles from Abingdon. Pass through Clifton Hampden, cross over the lovely arched bridge, and proceed straight ahead for about one mile before taking the right hand bend into Long Wittenham. Park near the entrance to St. Mary's Church (H.N.1).

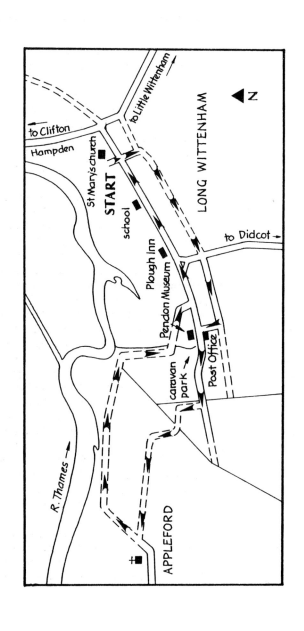

The walk: The church is well worth visiting and of particular interest is the extremely fine 12th century lead font. Immediately in front of the church cross over the main street onto a track between two houses and after a few yards turn right along the wide path known locally as Fieldside. In the distance you can see Wittenham Clumps (H.N.2). Continue along Fieldside passing some lovely houses and the back of the Vine public house until you reach the main road again. Cross over the road and take the concrete road directly in front of you which is marked by a footpath sign. After about 200 yards turn right and then turn left just past the Post Office. Very shortly you come to the Pendon Museum of Miniature Landscape and Transport (H.N.3) on your righthand side. The walk then continues straight ahead past a small caravan park ignoring a footpath to your right. This short stretch of the walk may be muddy after rain. The ubiquitous cooling towers of Didcot Power Station are now directly ahead of you. After about 200 yards you reach a single dead tree where you turn right into a field following the line of a stream which you should keep to your right. To the left on the horizon is Appleford Church towards which you are heading. At the end of the field turn left still keeping the stream on your right and turn right over a small bridge. You now continue along a path with a fence on your left and a hedgerow on your right. Follow the path through a gate. At this point the path runs parallel with the Thames which is a short distance away to your right. The track continues for approximately half a mile through pleasant countryside and takes you to Appleford Church (H.N.4). If you wish to visit this church consult the notice in the porch about how to obtain the keys.

After visiting the church retrace your steps for a few hundred yards to a point where the track divides. Take the left hand fork and make for the river passing a Sea Scouts' training ship on your left. On the opposite side of the river you can see the buildings of the JET Laboratory at Culham.

To continue the walk proceed by the side of the river, crossing a stile, until you come to a gate. Pass through the gate and turn right, away from the river keeping the fence on your righthand side. Head towards a stile at the far end of the field. Cross over the stile and turn right keeping a little stream on your left. After a few steps you reach another stile which you cross before passing over a bridge to your left. You now follow the path for about 100 yards and then turn left at another footbridge. Continue ahead noting the signals of the Pendon Museum on your right. You soon arrive at a narrow grassy lane and you pass between two white posts. When you reach the road turn left and this brings you back again to the main street of Long Wittenham. In the main street on your left you will find the Plough public house, Witta's Ham (H.N.5) (between the village hall and the school), the old village pound, and the church where you started your walk.

Historical Notes

H.N.1
Nothing now remains of the original wooden churches built by the Saxons in Long Wittenham. The present beautiful church was built by the Norman Lord of the Manor, Walter Giffard, third earl of Buckingham in about the year 1120. It then consisted only of a short chancel and a long aisleless nave and there have, of course, been many additions and modifications to the structure over the centuries. The church contains a magnificent 12th century lead font which stands on a large stone base. During the English Civil Wars the church wardens surrounded the font with a wooden case, packed with rubbish to hide it from Cromwell's soldiers in order to prevent it from being melted down and used for bullets. The font remained hidden in this fashion for nearly 200 years until 1839 when it was discovered and restored by the vicar. The table nearby on which the Roll of Honour of those killed in World War I is placed, is made from the case in which the font was concealed for so many years. A booklet providing a concise history of St. Mary's and entitled *A Guide to St. Mary's Church, Long Wittenham* is on sale in the church.

H.N.2
Castle Hill and Harp Hill are the two highest of the Sinodun Hills which are also known as the Wittenham Clumps after the trees at their summits. It is known that Castle Hill was fortified in the 8th

century during a war between the West Saxons and King Offa of Mercia. From the top of Wittenham Clumps you can gain a tremendous view of the Thames as it cuts an unlikely pattern through the plain.

H.N.3
The Pendon Museum of Miniature Landscape and Transport presents historically accurate miniature village and landscape scenes of the 1930's and includes miniature railway systems. The scenes depict farms and thatched cottages grouped in a model village. All details of village architecture, railway systems and people have been extensively researched. Also on display is John Ahern's historic pioneering work "The Madder Valley" and a collection of railway relics.

The museum is open all year round but the opening times and days are as follows: March to October: Saturdays, Sundays, and Bank Holidays 2pm-6pm; November to February: Saturdays and Sundays only 2pm-5pm. Admission prices: Adults 60p, Children 40p. Enquiries to Pendon Museum Trust Limited, Long Wittenham, Abingdon, Oxon. Tel. Clifton Hampden (086 730) 7365.

H.N.4
Prehistoric and Roman remains have been found at Appleford including a remarkable find of 22 pieces of Romano-British pewter. During the Civil Wars the inhabitants of Appleford, together with those of Sutton Courtenay, repelled a troop of Royalist cavalry commanded by Prince Rupert. The bells of the church include some of the first to be cast in the Wokingham foundry.

H.N.5
Witta was a Saxon who settled in the district in the 6th century and the village was named after him — "Witta's ham".

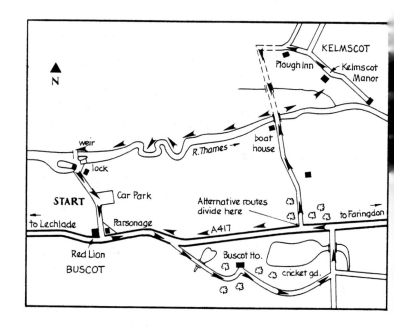

Buscot House and Park, and Kelmscot

Introduction: The highlight of this circular walk is Buscot House and Grounds with its 55-acre park, delightful water gardens and lake. The walk also takes you past Kelmscot Manor, the home of William Morris for 25 years. In addition it includes a pleasant stroll by the side of the River Thames. This walk must coincide with the opening hours of Buscot House and Park, since without this stretch of the route one's enjoyment of the walk as a whole will be lost. See H.N.2 for hours of opening. The full walk is slightly more difficult and longer than other walks in this volume but is certainly within the capability of families used to walking. The riverside section is unsuitable for pushchairs and buggies, although the rest of the walk is along good paths. As an alternative, we have suggested a much shorter and easier route of about two miles.

Distance: The complete circuit is 4¾ miles and about four hours should be sufficient time to do the walk, visit Buscot House, and stop for refreshments.

Refreshments: The Red Lion at Buscot near the car park, and the Plough Inn at Kelmscot both serve bar snacks and have beer gardens. Tea and light refreshments are served in the cafe within the grounds of Buscot House during July and August and at weekends.

How to get there: From Faringdon take the A417 road to Lechlade and turn right into the village of Buscot. Park at Buscot Weir Car Park about 200 yards from the main road.

The walk: Turn left out of the car park and proceed along the road, passing Buscot Parsonage (H.N.1) and the old pump, until you reach the main A417 Faringdon to Lechlade road. Turn left and walk along a footpath on the lefthand side of the road for about half a mile until you arrive at the main entrance to Buscot House and Park (H.N.2). Proceed up the main driveway passing over a bridge and there is a beautiful lake to your left where you may catch a glimpse of black swans. The main driveway climbs gently up to the house and in Spring you can see clusters of daffodils and primroses along the grassy banks and wooded areas. It is also possible to see and hear peacocks as you near the house.

After visiting the House and water gardens turn left outside the main entrance and walk down the road through the avenue of trees. When you reach the bottom of the hill, it is worth pausing a while to look back and appreciate the delightful 18th century architecture of the house. Continue along the road for about half a mile until you reach the cricket ground and pavilion on your left. Turn left at the crossroads and continue along the metalled road, and shortly you reach a bridge. To your left there is an attractive lake. Turn left at the main road and take the footpath on the lefthand side of the road. (Those wishing to take the shortened version of the walk should proceed along the footpath, past the main gates to Buscot House and back to the car park). However, those wishing to complete the full walk should continue along the path for only about 200 yards looking out for a public footpath along a track on the right marked by a cul-de-sac sign. This track leads up an incline away from the main road by the side of some woods. Take this track and after a few hundred yards turn round to gain further glimpses of Buscot House in the distance.

After approximately one mile you come to a gate. Pass through the gate and proceed straight ahead through a car park, over a wooden bridge, and past a small boathouse by the side of the Thames. You cross over the river by means of a wooden bridge just past the boathouse, and turn right and follow a path by the side of the river for about 300 yards. You then bear left across a field towards a gate. Pass through this gate and walk along the drive which brings you to Kelmscot Manor (H.N.3), the home of

William Morris from 1871 to 1896. The driveway leads to a road where you turn left and head towards the village of Kelmscot with its lovely old Cotswold stone houses. Proceed through the village, and just past the Plough Inn you turn left onto a track. After about 100 yards you bear right and continue along this track until you reach a further track which runs along by the side of a field on your left. Turn left along this track keeping the hedge on your left hand side. At the far end of the field you cross a bridge and a stile and follow the path straight ahead back to the river and the wooden bridge which you crossed earlier on.

Do not cross the bridge but continue right along by the side of the river passing over a stile and through a gate. You now continue walking by the river for approximately one mile passing through two gates and by the side of a pill box until you reach a wooden bridge just before Buscot Lock and Weir. Do not cross this bridge but carry on until you reach the weir and lock which can be traversed by a series of bridges and walkways. You soon come to a small pathway between two houses and at the end of this pathway you turn left onto a metalled road. Proceed along this road for about half a mile until you reach the car park again.

Historical Notes

H.N.1

Buscot Old Parsonage is an early 18th century house built of Cotswold stone, with a small garden. It is owned by the National Trust and is open all year but on Wednesdays only, 2pm-6pm, by appointment in writing with the Tenant, Buscot Old Parsonage, Faringdon. Admission price 40p. Enquiries to the National Trust Regional Office, Hughenden Manor, High Wycombe, Buckinghamshire HP14 4LA.

H.N.2

Buscot House was built by Edward Lovedon Townsend in 1870 in the then popular Adam style. The house is set on high ground at the centre of a landscaped park with a formal Italianate water garden linking the house and a lake covering an area of 22 acres. Buscot house contains some beautiful furniture and the important

51

Faringdon Collection of paintings. The collection was formed by the first Lord Faringdon who bought the estate in 1889. The collection includes an outstanding Rembrandt portrait, and works by Murillo, Gainsborough, and Reynolds. It also contains the Burn-Jones "Briar Rose" series of paintings which are located in the saloon and which were bought from the artist especially for this room in 1890. Buscot House is owned by the National Trust which also owns most of Buscot village, farmlands and woods running down to the Thames, and Buscot Weir.

The Park is open from 1st April to 30th September Wednesday, Thursday and Friday (including Good Friday) 2pm-6pm, and the 2nd and 4th Saturdays and following Sundays in each of these months (from 2pm-6pm). Admission price: House and Garden Adults £1.20p and children 60p. Gardens only Adults 60p and children 30p. Last admission to house 5.30pm. Enquiries to Estate Office, Buscot Park, Faringdon (Tel. Faringdon 20786).

H.N.3

The Elizabethan Kelmscot Manor was the home of William Morris (1834-96) the poet, artist, decorator, craftsman, designer, social reformer and printer. Morris originally shared the lease of the house with the Pre-Raphaelite painter Rosetti who shared a great passion for Morris' beautiful wife Jane. The three moved to Kelmscot in 1871 but Rosetti considered life at the manor to be dull and he returned to London in 1874. Morris regarded Kelmscot as his "heaven on earth" and continued to live at the manor until his death. He is buried in the local churchyard.

Kelmscot Manor is only open to the public occasionally during the summer.

Littlecote House, Roman Villa and Frontier City

Introduction: This walk is not of course in Oxfordshire but in Wiltshire. However we have included it because it is so close to the Oxfordshire border and provides quite outstanding facilities for a family outing. As well as enjoying a splendid walk in the heart of the Kennet Valley you can visit Littlecote House (H.N.1), a fine example of Tudor architecture, the Roman Villa (H.N.2) which has the largest Roman mosaic on permanent exhibition in Britain, and Frontier City (H.N.3), a replica Wild West town of the 1880's, where you can see gun fights and live shows which simulate cameos from American history.

The walk skirts the boundaries of Littlecote Park and grounds, but if you merely wish to enjoy a pleasant stroll then it is possible to retrace your steps once you have reached West Lodge (see map opposite and instructions below).

Distance: The circular walk is 3½ miles in length (or approximately 1½ miles if you return to Littlecote House when you reach West Lodge). The walk should take a little over two hours to complete but naturally you need to allow considerably longer to visit the House, Villa and Frontier City.

Refreshments: There are excellent tea rooms adjacent to the House which sell hot and cold drinks, sandwiches and homemade cakes.

How to get there: The simplest way is by car from Hungerford where you take the A419 (from the A4) for about two miles. You turn off on the Froxfield road towards Littlecote about half a mile

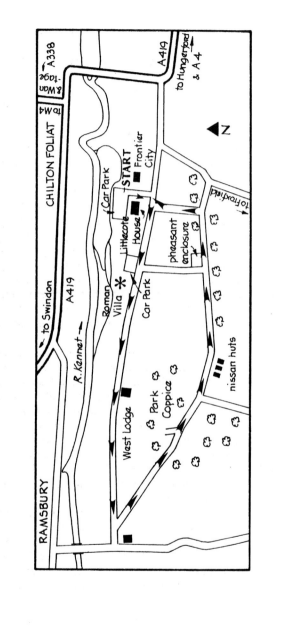

before the village of Chilton Foliat. You continue along this road for about half a mile and turn right through the main gates of Littlecote Park. Proceed down the main drive passing through a beautiful avenue of trees and turn right into the free car park.

The walk: Rejoin the main driveway and turn right following the arrows towards the Roman excavations. As you pass in front of Littlecote House stop at the wrought iron gates and admire the magnificent south front facade. When you reach the Roman Villa car park the road bends towards the left but you continue straight ahead through a green metal gate (marked with a public footpath sign). You now traverse the edge of a field keeping a fence to your right, and you pass the archaeological site also on your right. Shortly you reach a point where the path forks and you continue straight ahead along the side of the field ignoring the track to your right. You are now walking through an area of magnificent countryside and you can catch glimpses of the River Kennet to your right as you walk along. In the summer the overgrown areas of this stretch of the walk are alive with a colourful array of butterflies.

After about another half mile or so you come to a gate and beyond this a lovely home known as West Lodge (note the majestic oak tree to your right just before you reach the gate). At this point those not wishing to complete the full walk can retrace their steps back to the car park. But to continue the walk pass through the gate and proceed along a track with the river on your right. You continue ahead for about 500 yards passing through beautiful rolling countryside until you reach a bridleway sign on your left just before some houses. Take the bridleway and continue up an incline into some woods, admiring the splendours of the Kennet Valley to your left.

When you reach the top of the hill ignore a righthand fork and continue straight on along a path which soon bears right then left along the edge of a beech and oak wood. After a few hundred yards you emerge from the wood onto a concrete road. Turn right and continue downhill for about 200 yards until the road divides. Here you bear left along a concrete road past a small wood on the right. Soon you reach a group of three old Nissen huts and you can now see Littlecote House again to your left.

Follow the road round to the left and continue for about a third of a mile until you reach a junction. Proceed straight ahead up the hill ignoring the lefthand turn. You soon pass by a pheasant enclosure on your left and a few hundred yards later you turn left along a metalled road following signposts marked Littlecote House. This road brings you back to Littlecote House and the start of the walk.

Historical Notes

H.N.1

Littlecote House and Roman Villa are open from April until September on Saturdays, Sundays and Bank Holidays, 2pm-6pm, and from July to September they are open weekdays 2pm-5pm. Admission to the House costs: £1.20 for adults and 70p for children. The admission prices for the Roman Villa are: adults 60p and children 40p. Dogs are not allowed in the Roman Villa. For information regarding opening times, parties, bookings, teas etc. Tel. 048 86 2170 or 048 86 2509 (weekends and evenings Tel. 048 86 2528).

Littlecote House is a magnificent Tudor mansion surrounded by attractive gardens and parkland. It was built ca. 1490-1520 by the Darrell family and was later owned by the famous Popham family. Many royal visitors have been entertained at Littlecote including Henry VIII, Elizabeth I, Charles II and George VI. The House has a superb Great Hall which contains a unique collection of militaria from the English Civil War period including bandoliers, helmets, armour and swords, and a good display of 17th century firearms. There is also a finger stock said to have been used by Judge Popham to confine prisoners to the dock, and the great 30 feet long Shovel-Board table. There are also moulded ceilings, panelled rooms, fine tapestries, beautiful oak furniture, and a notorious haunted landing and bedroom!

H.N.2

The Roman Villa dates from the 1st to the early 5th century AD and includes the Littlecote Orpheus mosaic which may be claimed to be one of the most interesting so far discovered in England. The colourful mosaic forms the focal point of an extensive archaeological excavation covering some three acres.

H.N.3

Frontier City is open April-September, Saturdays, Sundays, and Bank Holidays from High Noon to 6pm, and from July to September weekdays High Noon to 5pm. The admission prices are: Adults £1 and children 80p. You can see live shows and shootouts as well as a Wells Fargo office, an undertaker's parlour, a saloon, sheriff's office and jail, a bank, general store and livery together with a Western museum and Sioux reservation.

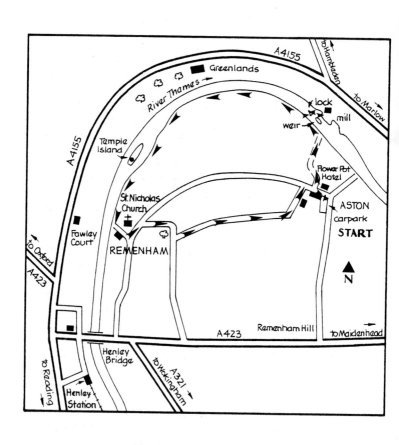

Henley-on-Thames, Aston and Hambleden Lock

Introduction: The attractions of this delightful family walk, which begins at the village of Aston, include Hambleden Lock, with its impressive weirs and mill buildings (H.N.1), Temple Island (H.N.2) and some truly magnificent Thames Valley scenery, as well as some marvellous views across to the Chiltern Beechwoods. Moreover, the family will also be able to visit Henley-on-Thames, home of the famous Royal Regatta (H.N.3), where in summer it is possible to enjoy a riverside picnic or a boating expedition. In Henley you can park by the river just south of the town centre quite near the railway station. Near the car park is a pleasant public park with fairground rides (in summer), swings, slides, and public tennis courts. Alternatively, there is a more central car park beyond the Town Hall off King's Road.

Three places near Henley which are also worth visiting are: Greys Court to the west, an Elizabethan manor house owned by the National Trust; Stonor to the northwest, a family house and a centre for Recusancy since the 1580s which has a beautiful deer park and beechwoods; and to the northeast the pretty Chiltern village of Hambleden with its fine church and manor house.

Distance: The circuit is about three miles and almost all of the chosen route is along flat terrain. Allow yourself two hours both to complete the walk in a leisurely fashion and to pause awhile at Hambleden Weir.

Refreshments: At the start of the walk there is the Flower Pot Hotel which has a beer garden, and in Henley itself, of course, there are several good public houses, cafes and tea rooms.

How to get there: By car from Henley cross the bridge over the Thames and take the A423 Maidenhead road. After about a mile at Remenham Hill take a left turn to the village of Aston where you may park opposite the Flower Pot Hotel.

The walk: Turn left out of the car park, past the telephone box with the Flower Pot Hotel on your right (i.e., take the road to Remenham). After a few paces you turn right at a public footpath sign opposite the entrance to Aston Farm. Pass through the grey gates and continue along the track for about a quarter of a mile until you reach the River Thames. As you walk down the track enjoying the beautiful Thames Valley countryside you can see The Temple on Temple Island to your left which you will pass at a later stage of the walk. When you arrive at the Thames turn left and follow the path along the river bank and very shortly you come to Hambleden Lock. Here it is worth an enjoyable diversion — cross over the lock and take the extensive walkways over the weir to Hambleden Mill. It should be noted that the walkways are safe as long as young children are properly supervised and controlled and dogs are kept on a leash.

After visiting the mill retrace your steps, cross back over the lock, turn right and go through the gate at the far end. You now continue along the Thames and as you follow the curve of the river you will notice on your right the splendid white facade and magnificent grounds of Greenlands (H.N.4). The walking is easy along the metalled footpath and as the river straightens out you can see directly in front of you in the distance the famous bridge (H.N.5) at Henley. After a few minutes walking you reach Temple Island with its pillared temple marking the end of the regatta course.

Just past Temple Island on your left you will see a red-brick house known as Remenham Manor with its croquet lawn, and a little further a more modern dwelling called River House. Immediately after you have passed by River House turn sharp left and cross the stile adjacent to a green gate. Continue ahead for about 150 yards and walk by the side of a large black gate and then continue to St. Nicholas's Church at Remenham (H.N.6), a few yards ahead.

At the end of the lane past the church turn left along a quiet road and after a hundred yards or so you reach a junction and a signpost. Here you turn right up the hill in the direction marked Maidenhead. As you climb you can look down to the stretch of the Thames Valley along which you have just walked.

Continue on the road through a small copse. When you emerge from the copse carry on for about 20 yards and take a track on your left (the public footpath sign marking this track is almost hidden in the hedge). You will now see a football pitch on your right. As you proceed along the track there are some really pleasant views down to the Thames and beyond to the beechwoods around Hambleden. After about half a mile the track bears left and descends to the road through a small wood. On reaching the road turn right and pass by the entrance to Aston Lodge and then the building where sixteen Oxfordshire artists and craftsmen have their studio. After about 100 yards you arrive back at the car park where the walk commenced.

Historical Notes

H.N.1
Hambleden Mill, which dates from 1338, has now been converted into private residences. The nearby weir is popular with canoeists while the stretch of river near the lock is a favourite haunt of anglers.

H.N.2
The English architect, James Wyatt (1746-1813) worked at Fawley Court (on the opposite side of the Thames from Remenham) in 1771 at which time he designed the Temple with its decorative cupola on what became known as Temple Island. The Temple was the principal northeast vista from Fawley Court which is now a business studies centre. Wyatt, who worked on cathedral restorations at Salisbury, Durham and elsewhere also completed the Radcliffe Observatory, Oxford, between 1776 and 1794.

H.N.3

The first Oxford and Cambridge University Boat Race was held on 10th June 1829 when the two crews raced between Hambleden Lock and Henley Bridge. Ten years later on 14th June 1839 the first annual Henley Regatta took place. In 1851 Prince Albert became the patron of the regatta and thereafter it became known as the Royal Henley Regatta and it took its place in the London season. Nowadays the regatta extends from Temple Island to opposite the Phyllis Court Club a little below Henley Bridge. The Regatta, which is held during the first week in July, has no official status in international rowing although it is generally recognized as an important event in the sporting and social calendars, and attracts good crews from overseas.

H.N.4

This beautifully situated mansion was rebuilt in the Italian style principally in 1871 by W.H. Smith, the founder of the firm of booksellers. However, a house has existed near this site for centuries. For example, in 1480 a property stood here which belonged to Sir William Stonor of Stonor Park. The house was then situated well below the present building on the north bank where the river sweeps round above Hambleden Lock. During the Civil War Greenlands, which had been fortified in May 1644 by its owner, the Royalist Sir John D'Oyley, withstood a siege which lasted six months. Several cannon balls were dug up in the grounds in 1853. Today the building is used as an Administrative Staff College.

H.N.5

The present Henley Bridge was constructed in 1786 to the design of William Hayward. It is built of stone and has two carved heads on the keystones. One faces downstream and represents Thamesis and the other faces upstream and represents Isis. There have been bridges across the Thames at this point since the 13th century.

H.N.6

Remenham in Anglo-Saxon is said to mean "Home of the Raven" but the word may also mean "Home of the Remi", the Remi being a Celtic tribe. A church is believed to have existed here in 1066 and the parish was mentioned in the Domesday Book in 1086. Originally the parish was a Chapelry of Hurley and was served by the monks of Hurley Priory. Two restorations of the church took place in 1838 and 1870 which led to the destruction of the greater part of the ancient building. The South Aisle was added in 1870. There are several interesting features of the church including: a pair of iron gates at the front of the South Aisle which were hand wrought in Siena in 1873 and which were presented to the church by John Noble of Park Place; some medieval tiles around the pulpit which were probably the work of Chiltern tile-makers; the beautifully carved Lych Gate which was placed there in memory of Violet Constance Noble who died of scarlet fever at the age of 14; and close to the main entrance the grave of Caleb Gould, a lock-keeper who died in 1836 at the age of 92, which bears the words of the poet Gray:

"This world's a jest,
  And all things show it,
  I thought so once,
  But now I know it".